SUPER SPEED

GO-KART Racing

BY TRACY NELSON MAURER

Reading Consultant:
Barbara J. Fox
Professor Emerita
North Carolina State University

Content Consultant:
Donald Davidson
Historian, Indianapolis Motor Speedway
Indianapolis, Indiana

CAPSTONE PRESS
a capstone imprint

Blazers Books are published by Capstone Press,
1710 Roe Crest Drive, North Mankato, Minnesota 56003
www.capstonepub.com

Library of Congress Cataloging-in-Publication Data
Maurer, Tracy, 1965–
    Go-kart racing / by Tracy Nelson Maurer.
    p. cm.—(Blazers. super speed)
    Includes bibliographical references and index.
    Summary: "Describes go-karts and kart racing, including safety features and rules
governing kart races"—Provided by publisher.
    ISBN 978-1-4296-9998-3 (library binding)
    ISBN 978-1-4765-1361-4 (ebook pdf)
1. Karting—Juvenile literature. I. Title.
GV1029.5.M43 2013
796.7'6—dc23   2012033230

Editorial Credits
Aaron Sautter, editor; Kyle Grenz, designer; Eric Manske, production specialist

Photo Credits
AP Images: The Indianapolis Star/Greg Griffo, 29; Dreamstime: 36clicks/Corepics Vor, 16–17,
Chirnoaga, 26–27, Enjoylife25/Eric Gevaert, 15, Gunter Nezhoda, 21, Jaggat, 24–25; Getty Images:
Source Interlink Media/Bob D'Olivo, 6–7; Newscom: Design Pics/SICI, 14, Heiner Heine Image Broker,
22, Nice Matin/PhotoPQR/Eric Duliere, 9, 12–13, SIPA/Jean-Philippe Pariente, 23, ZUMA Press/
MAXPPP/Denis Lambert, cover; Shutterstock: Gunter Nezhoda, 18–19, Jaggat, 4–5, TachePhoto, 11

Artistic Effects
Shutterstock: 1xpert, My Portfolio, rodho

Printed in the United States of America in Brainerd, Minnesota.
092012   006938BANGS13

TABLE OF CONTENTS

SMALL KARTS, BIG FUN

The crackling sound of small **engines** fills the air. A green flag waves, and go-karts launch from the starting line. These speedy machines deliver big fun!

engine—a machine in which fuel burns to provide power

Go-kart racing began after World War II
(1939–1945). In the 1950s hundreds of
companies were building karts. Today less
than 10 companies build most karts used
around the world.

FAST FACT

Karts used by professional drivers reach speeds of more than 160 miles (257 kilometers) per hour.

KART DESIGN

Karts don't need big engines to move fast. The karts' small size, low weight, and low position give them incredible speed. Smooth racing **slicks** help keep karts from spinning out on the track.

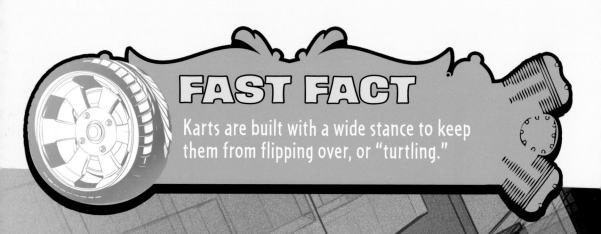

FAST FACT

Karts are built with a wide stance to keep them from flipping over, or "turtling."

slick—a racing tire made with a smooth, soft
surface to get a strong grip on the track

Nimble touch-and-go (TaG) karts use just one forward **gear**. Shifter karts have up to six gears. SuperKarts have the most powerful engines. They can travel up to 160 miles (257 km) per hour.

Touch and Go (TaG) Kart
- push-button starter
- engine size: 125 cubic centimeters (cc)
- top speed: 115 mph (185 kph)

Shifter Kart
- six gears
- engine size: 125cc
- top speed: 125 mph (201 kph)

SuperKart
- six gears
- engine size: 250cc
- top speed: 160 mph (257 kph)

mph—miles per hour

kph—kilometers per hour

FAST FACT

Shifter kart drivers often shift gears more than 20 times per lap. Drivers shift gears to slow down around turns and to gain speed on straight parts of a track.

GEAR SHIFTER

gear—a toothed wheel that fits into another toothed wheel; gears transfer power from an engine to a vehicle's tires to make it move

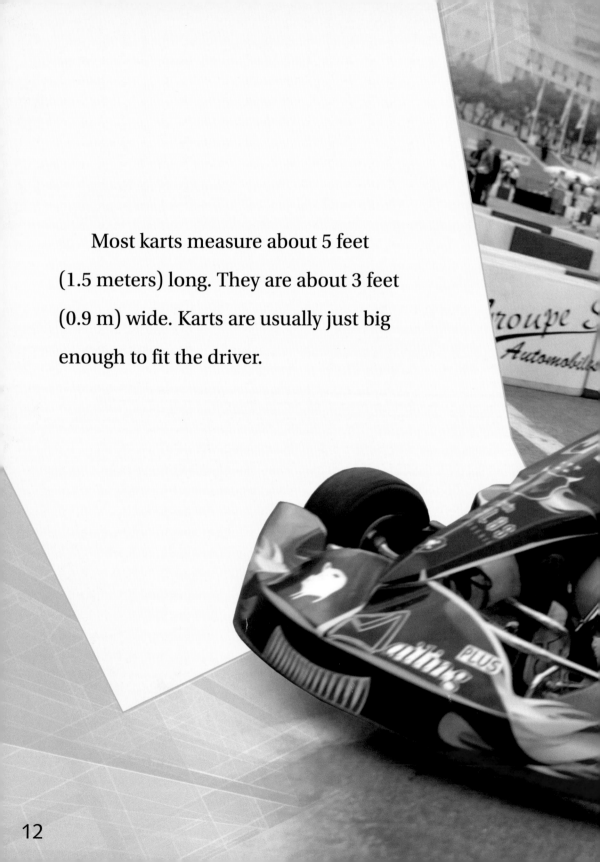

Most karts measure about 5 feet (1.5 meters) long. They are about 3 feet (0.9 m) wide. Karts are usually just big enough to fit the driver.

FAST FACT

Some karts have a longer "limo" design for drivers over 6 feet (183 centimeters) tall.

All karts sit less than 2 inches (5 cm) above the track. This position helps lower **wind resistance** so karts can move faster.

wind resistance—the force of air that pushes against a moving object

FAST FACT

Some adult karts can zoom from 0 to 60 miles (0 to 97 km) per hour in only four seconds!

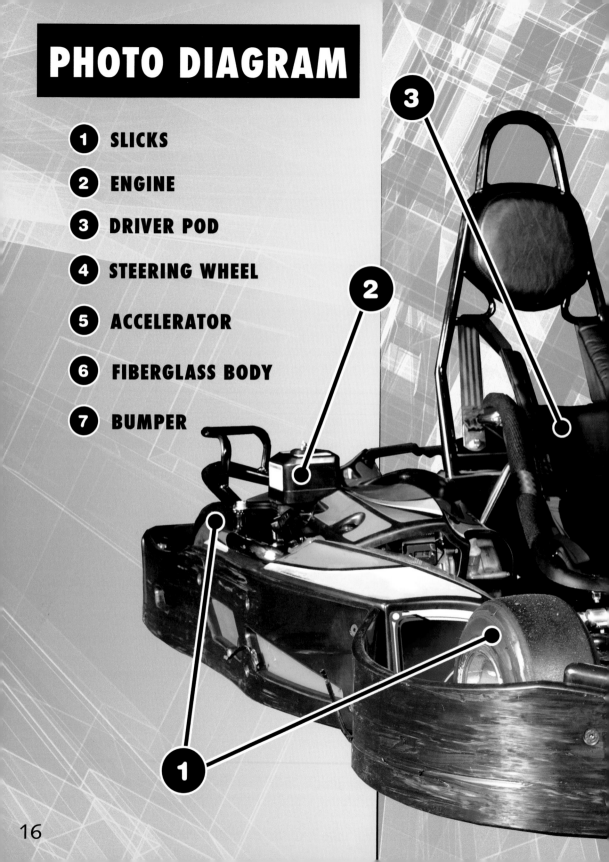

PHOTO DIAGRAM

1. SLICKS
2. ENGINE
3. DRIVER POD
4. STEERING WHEEL
5. ACCELERATOR
6. FIBERGLASS BODY
7. BUMPER

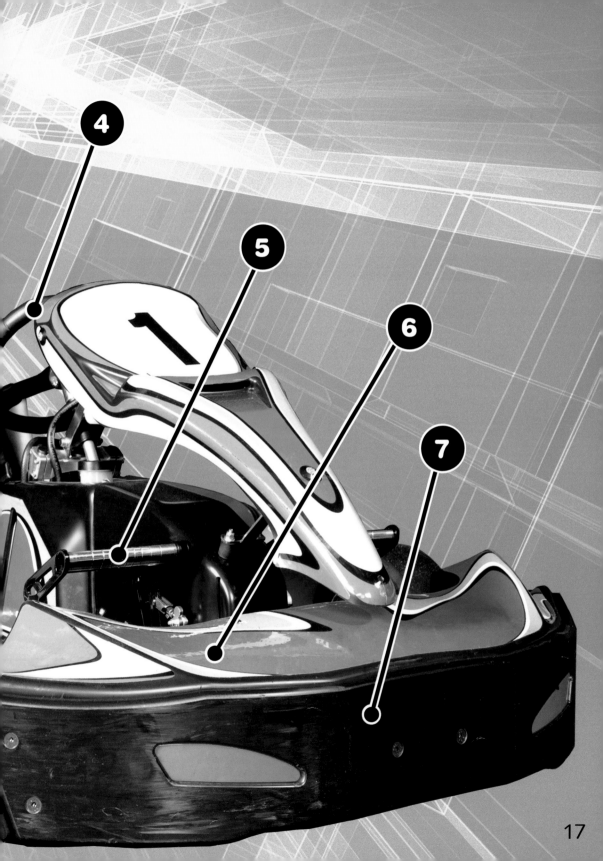

HELMET

NECK BRACE

CHEST PROTECTOR

RACING SUIT

GLOVES

Some karts do not have seat belts. Drivers often prefer to be flung away from their machines in an accident. Drivers wear a full-face helmet, **neck brace**, and racing suit for protection.

neck brace—a safety device worn to protect a driver's neck in case of a crash

AT THE TRACK

Kart racers drive in one of several classes. The classes are based on a driver's age and experience. Classes are also based on kart type or racetrack style.

FAST FACT

Drivers may need to add special weights to their karts. The weights make sure all the racers and their karts weigh the same.

Many kart tracks are shaped like simple ovals. Small sprint tracks often have many tight turns. Road races take place on long, twisty enduro tracks.

Enduro tracks are usually more than 1.5 miles (2.4 km) long.

FAST FACT

Some tracks have lights for night racing. Others are indoors so races can be run in any weather.

Kart drivers must control their karts at all times during races. They take care not to hit other karts. Drivers watch for openings to pass other karts and take the lead.

FAST FACT

Jerking the steering wheel while driving too fast can cause a kart to spin out of control.

TRACK FLAGS

GREEN

START THE RACE.

YELLOW

CAUTION! WATCH FOR AN ACCIDENT OR SPIN OUT. NO PASSING IS ALLOWED.

BLUE

LET THE FASTER KART PASS.

RED

STOP RACING AND PULL OFF THE COURSE.

WHITE

ONE LAP TO GO.

BLACK

A RACER HAS BROKEN A RULE AND MUST LEAVE THE RACE.

CHECKERED

THE RACE IS OVER.

Each class, track, and racing organization has different rules. Bumping other karts is against the rules at most tracks. Racers can be **disqualified** for breaking the rules.

disqualify—to remove someone from a race because he or she has broken the rules

JUST THE START

Kart racing can be a fun hobby.
It can also lead to a professional racing
career. Some drivers move on to race
powerful stock cars or other race cars.
Kart racing delivers big-time fun!

career—the type of work a person does

FAST FACT

Drivers in the National Association for Stock Car Auto Racing (NASCAR) often enjoy racing karts in their free time.

GLOSSARY

career (ka-REER)—the type of work a person does

disqualify (dis-KWAH-luh-fye)—to remove someone from a race because he or she has broken the rules

engine (EN-juhn)—a machine in which fuel burns to provide power

gear (GEER)—a toothed wheel that fits into another toothed wheel; gears transfer power from an engine to a vehicle's tires to make it move

neck brace (NEK BRAYS)—a safety device worn to protect a driver's neck in case of a crash

slick (SLIK)—a racing tire made with a smooth, soft surface to get a strong grip on the track

stance (STANS)—the way a kart's wheels are positioned; a wide stance helps keep a kart from flipping over

wind resistance (WIND ri-ZISS-tuhnss)—the force of air that pushes against a moving object; wind resistance increases with an object's speed

READ MORE

David, Jack. *Go-Kart Racing.* Action Sports. Minneapolis: Bellwether Media, 2008.

Mason, Paul. *Karting.* Motorsports. Mankato, Minn.: Amicus, 2011.

Norville, Alison G. *Kart Racers.* Kid Racers. Berkeley Heights, N.J.: Enslow Publishers, 2010.

INTERNET SITES

FactHound offers a safe, fun way to find Internet sites related to this book. All of the sites on FactHound have been researched by our staff.

Here's all you do:

Visit *www.facthound.com*

Type in this code: 9781429699983

 Check out projects, games and lots more at **www.capstonekids.com**

INDEX